*My Soul Is
From a
Different
Place*

Cherie Burbach

My Soul Is From a Different Place

Cherie Burbach

Bonjour Publishing

Cherie Burbach

My Soul Is From a Different Place

All rights reserved.

Copyright © 2014 by Cherie Burbach
MY SOUL IS FROM A DIFFERENT PLACE

Cover art by Cherie Burbach

All rights reserved. No part of this book may be reproduced by an mechanical, photographic, or electronic process, or in the form of a photographic recording; nor may it be stored in a retrieval system, transmitted, or otherwise be copied for public or private use - other than for "fair use" as brief quotations embodied in articles and reviews without prior written permission of the publisher. In the event you use any of the information in this book for yourself, the author and the publisher assume no responsibility for your actions.

ISBN 978-0-9834750-6-4
Printed in the United States of America

My Soul Is From a Different Place

Also by Cherie Burbach

Nonfiction

21 Simple Things You Can Do To Help Someone With Diabetes

Internet Dating Is Not Like Ordering a Pizza

21 Ways to Promote Your Book on Twitter

Poetry

Father's Eyes

The Difference Now

A New Dish

New and Selected Poems

Yes, You

Cherie Burbach

My Soul Is From a Different Place

*For my husband,
thank you for ten beautiful years.*

Cherie Burbach

My Soul Is From a Different Place

> *"My soul is from a different place,*
> *it remembers the day*
> *God placed it gently within this body*
> *that had yet to form."*
>
> *~ Cherie Burbach*

Cherie Burbach

Table of Contents

life, love, loss.................................15

Cardinal...16

The Wise Bride 18

Each Time You Smile 20

Early Morning Choir 21

Called 22

Shallow..23

Afternoon Cinema 25

Those Who Explain 27

You Should Know..............................29

This House Had 30

A Cloak of Forgiveness 32

The Basket...35

Finite 40

A Selfish Act......................................42

Waste...43

Robin's Nest 45

The Girl I Wanted to Be 49

faith, hope, grace 53

- *The Purpose of Pain* 54
- *Kiss That Scar* 56
- *Our Beautiful Brokenness* 58
- *The Smile* 61
- *What Is Prayer?* 62
- *No Suffering in Heaven* 64
- *High Regard* 66
- *Beacon* 68
- *Call to Me* 70
- *The Blessing In My Sleepless Night* 72
- *Free Pass* 74
- *Every Jagged Edge* 76
- *You Have Seen Us Through* 79
- *This Is What I Crave* 82
- *I See God* 84
- *My Soul Is From a Different Place* 86

My Soul Is From a Different Place

Cherie Burbach

life,

love,

loss

Cardinal

Red feathers stand out defiantly
against snow heavy branches.
He sits boldly,
refusing to hide
while she perches near him
quietly but strong.

As danger approaches,
he releases a sound,
sharp and searing,
a proclamation
that lets the world know
he is here
and he may move about
to protect himself
but he will not leave.

He is here to guard over her,
and the little ones hidden away.
He is here to
draw oohs and ahhs
as a handmade creation by God.

My Soul Is From a Different Place

He might face danger,
and the cruelness of winter,
but he will raise his voice
to celebrate the joy of life
and to those who find him
irritating, too brash, and lacking grace
he will simply fly
to a higher branch
and continue his
own personal song.

The Wise Bride

I tied my shame to a post
then ran as far and as fast
as I could
until I was breathless,

hands on knees
drinking in
deep pockets of air
like the sweetest tea.

Each failure
and embarrassment
knotted tightly together
with my best ribbon.

Each step had pulled
that ribbon tight
until there were miles
between me and that post.

My shame hung up like
clothes on a laundry line
waving easily in the wind.
Each piece colorful, unique.

My Soul Is From a Different Place

As I looked back
at the display
my past mistakes created
I saw truth, beauty, and growth.

I felt them tug at my body
this ribbon still anchored
to my past at one end
and my present life at the other.

I could cut them loose and run,
leave them flying wildly to get lost,
landing on others who don't
know what to do with them.

Or I could go back
let them wind their way around me
over and over,
so tight that I can't breathe.

Instead, I tug, hard,
and the ribbon comes free from the poll
my mistakes and shame
fly openly behind me

like the train of a
beautiful wedding dress
worn by me,
the wise bride.

Each Time You Smile

There is a ray
of sunlight
that shines brighter
each time
you smile.

Early Morning Choir

The birds chirp mightily
through the dark morning hours,
urging the sun
out from its hiding place.

They call out
for warmth, guidance,
over their natural world
and perhaps over ours as well.

They remain steadfast
assured each day
that they will see the sun,
never doubtful of its return.

Their hours of early morning work
are rewarded each day,
as the sun slowly warms their bodies,
offers light to guide their flight.

They sing happily
joyful at the rise
of the new day,
offering praise before they begin
the work that must be done.

Called

They called me stupid,
and slow.
My thoughts churned
while they taunted,
and I wished I could
change my introspective ways.

She called me a low life,
a disappointment.
My heart broke with
her words,
and I prayed that
she could see how
wrong she was,
and love me.

He called me His own,
His child.
My soul burst open
with happiness.
My longing
finally fulfilled.

Shallow

He looked
at her
and
sneered.

He saw lines on her face,
and wondered aloud
if she'd gone up
a size or two.

He expected her
to cry.
She always did,
so easily, it seemed.

She glanced at him,
barely
noticing him,
and looked away.

He ran
ahead of her,
blocking
her path.

He repeated his thoughts,
louder this time
and added,
"I see you've changed."

He chuckled,
wondering how
she looked
so much older.

She took in
his arrogant smirk.
"And I see
you haven't."

He felt satisfaction
at the thought
that she noticed
how good he looked.

And she smiled to herself,
knowing that's not
what she meant
at all.

Afternoon Cinema

We entered a room
with no doors or windows,
open to the world and our feelings,

open to the anger we felt,
at having our failures
displayed for all to see.

They played out before us,
and we watched,
rapt with attention,

like people with free tickets
to an afternoon cinema,
munching on our popcorn

entertained at the mistakes of others
but shocked
when our own came up on screen.

So when the showing was over,
we sat, disgusted and amazed
with each other.

How alike we were!
How similar
our regrets and shame.

And all we could do was nod,
and say to each other,
"I understand you."

My Soul Is From a Different Place

Those Who Explain

They'll explain away your pain,
those well-meaning people
who want to show you
about the world.

They'll tell you logical reasons
why you feel as you do,
as if they can ease the hurt
by sharing their opinion.

But feelings don't follow logic.
The hurt you feel might have started
years and years ago,
and what were you to do?
This hated act transformed into
a tiny seed that placed itself
into your heart.

When someone who
should have loved you unconditionally
did the unthinkable
and it tarnished your body and soul,
you didn't even realize
it at first, but as years
marched on
you gravitated toward the hurt,

searching for people and situations
that could make it seem normal.

When you found people
who made you feel just as bad,
you thanked them with your devotion.

You saved up your love for them.

This dysfunction was the nourishment
this little seed needed to root itself
firmly into your life,
until it towered over you
and became the one thing
people saw when they looked at you.

Then those same people,
who assumed you couldn't see
their judgment through their loud voices
and toothpaste smiles
told you logically
why you felt as you did.

Your pain became a conversation
topic between them.

You Should Know

You should know
that I love you
even now
after what you said and did
despite our short time together.

You should know
that I've forgiven us
you and me both
but I'm sad
over what we became.

You should know
that I've moved on
because I had to
but if you wanted to try again
I would.

This House Had

This house had
a puppy,
who filled this space
with joy, even as she
chewed our books
and furniture,

then grew to be
the family dog
who brought us smiles
and demonstrated
unconditional love.

This house had
a newly married couple
who loved and fought
and learned to cling
to God and each other,

who lived joyfully
and celebrated
a decade together
with genuine surprise
that time had flown so fast.

My Soul Is From a Different Place

This house had
homemade meals,
holiday memories,
family reunions,

and many, many
visits from friends,
all of whom
laughed and cried,
prayed and rejoiced.

This house had
all the people and pets
and faith and love
to make it
a home,
but it didn't have you.

A Cloak of Forgiveness

All I wanted
was an acknowledgement
of what happened
to hear the words "I'm sorry"
once.

That's all that was needed
so we could move on,
and start again.

An apology
not meant to condemn
or even to cause shame,
but to lay down
the blanket of wisdom
on our path
so we could walk freely
without treading on the past
stamping on the pain
that is always there
but lessened with prayer
and God's grace.

Words of apology
could be the barrier over that pain,
allowing us to walk and even run,

feet pounding over it
without it calling up the hurt
and making new cuts
in our mind and heart.

We could have had
a fresh start,
a new path to forge.

But words of apology
would never come.

Instead, more layers were added
to the path of pain,
denials thrown down
depths of rewritten history piled on,
so that the perpetrator wore the mask of the victim.

Each lie, a landmine,
hidden within the path
without logic,
so there was no way to avoid them
as we walked.

Some, kept in a pocket,
tossed in front of me
during times I would least expect,
so I'd be caught off guard,
stumbling to maintain my balance
as explosions erupted around me.

Sometimes, I'd foolishly forge on,
trying to run ahead,
ignoring the fire around me,
pretending my injuries
weren't really there.

Finally, after years of
fighting alone,
I reached up.
And He was there.

He'd been there, all along,
laying down a cloak of forgiveness
that I could cross
and enter a new path.
But I couldn't see Him then,
head bent so low in my own pain,
I never thought to look up.

But when I did,
the cool, soft path He offered
felt good on my feet.
The road ahead of me
was level,
and I could
safely walk
to my destiny
without explosive hatred
slowing me down.

The Basket

She heard someone at the door
and as she answered it
saw a basket on the doorstep.
A baby? She wondered.

She picked up the basket,
light as air,
and as she carried it inside,
noticed it was empty,
except for a note, which read,
"Your problems. Here."

She shook her head.
Read it again.
Folded the paper,
and put it back in the basket.

Problems?
She laughed,
then grabbed
the note again.

It was balled up,
the paper crinkled
from where she had
smashed it in her hand.

She smoothed it out,
read it again.
This time it said:
"Toss them in."

She dropped the paper,
tried to clear her thoughts.
What was this? A joke?
She shook her head again.

But she pictured her problems,
and picking up the paper again,
silently thought of each one.
Then she crumbled the paper
and tossed it into the basket.

She turned to go,
wanted to leave the paper
and the basket behind,
but struggled to walk away.

She reached for the paper again.
This time it read,
"Yes. Right here.
Don't worry.
I can hold them."

She got a little cocky.
Sure, sure, she thought,
I'll give you my problems!
Here!
She tossed the paper in the basket.

"Ready?" She asked sarcastically.
"Okay then, how about this?
My mortgage is overdue.
My husband took off,
and I can't make
ends meet by myself.
And I'm angry!
Is that a problem?
Because if it is,
you can take that, too."

She waited.
Folded her arms and frowned.
Finally she turned,
slammed the door on the basket
and went inside.

That night,
she slept,
fitfully, deeply.
The first time that had
happened in months.

As she woke,
she thought of the basket,
and ran to see
if it was still there.

My Soul Is From a Different Place

She opened the door,
and the basket now held
a bouquet of flowers.
She reached down
and smelled their
beautiful fragrance,
and smiled to herself,
and brought the basket
inside.

Finite

You wasted your breath
so finite in this life
whispering lies about me.

You felt the satisfaction
in my hurt
at your betrayal.

You spent your words
so finite in our years
speaking hatred about me.

You smiled every time
you heard me
suffer with sadness.

You prayed many prayers
asking God
to bring me down.

You spent these finite moments
pushing me away
while I tried to love you.

My Soul Is From a Different Place

I spent them with tears, wondering why,
until God lifted the cloak of shame
you put upon my shoulders.

And I could live joyfully
these finite years,
while you imagined me done.

A Selfish Act

Is it true?
You went to that dark place?
After all the lessons you learned here?

All the knowledge you gained from your mistakes,
how selfish that you
wouldn't share it.

How selfish that you
withheld your love
and left pain behind.

How selfish that after
God surrounded you
with people who loved you,

the way you chose
to reciprocate their love
was by leaving them…
all alone…

taking your apologies
and the affection you owed them
with you.

Waste

Waste of breath
to change the mind of someone
who tells lies about me
who never got to know me
who made up her mind about me
      before we even met.

I could point out the facts
that prove she is wrong,
but why?

Instead, I will use my breath
to sing the praises of God
to speak truth
to whisper "I love you"
to the one who stands by my side.

Waste of thought
to wonder why you never liked me
to go over every step I could have made
      that displeased you
to come up with yet another way
      I can try for your approval.

I could continue thinking
about your terrible treatment of me,
but why?

Instead, I will use my thoughts
to meditate on the blessings of God
to create words and pictures
        that champion beauty
to encourage others who
have someone like you in their life.

Waste of emotion
to cry over someone
who enjoys my misery
who doesn't want reconciliation
who has evoked pity from those
        who believe her false testimony.

I could cry for years and years more
over the brokenness of our relationship,
but I've done that already.

Instead, I will use my tears
to clear my vision so I can see you
        as you really are
to wash away the hurt of everything
        you have accused me of
to call up strength I didn't realize I had.

Robin's Nest

The robin sings
"Follow me.
I have a secret
to show you."

She leads me
to a doorway,
where above
sits her nest.

"Isn't it beautiful?"
From a distance,
it is the color of mud,
made with sticks and feathers.

Beautiful?
I shake my head.
"You need to look closely,"
she says, giving me a nudge.

I walk slowly towards it
and see eggs inside,
a brilliant color
of blue.

Their oval shape
set perfectly against
the sharp edges
of the nest.

I reach out
to touch them
and prick
my finger

on the edges
of a twig
that is hidden just
beneath the surface.

As I pull back my hand,
the robin says,
"I patterned this nest
after your heart.

See how you've
been hurt,
just trying to
get near it?

That's what happens
to the people
who try and
love you."

My Soul Is From a Different Place

I looked at the nest again,
sturdy and strong,
yet yielding to
the winds of change.

The nest, so plain,
it could blend in
with the background
had the robin chose to hide it.

Instead, it sat
proudly over my doorway,
welcoming everyone in
but using

the rough edges
to protect
its priceless contents
from those who would do harm.

"You can get close,"
she told me,
"with care
and gentleness."

I moved closer
enough to feel
the joy of a life
well loved.

The robin
sang her
song
in triumph.

The Girl I Wanted to Be

I protected the silence
like all who
shared your name,

wordlessly, instinctively,
our shame putting tape
over our mouths,

our fear binding our hands,
preventing them from
holding onto truth.

I performed my role
as a girl stepping into destiny
so cognizant of this

important task,
you convinced me that my
life depended on it.

I chased your approval
condition upon
your ever changing moods.

I turned to God, but felt His silence
as I asked Him to change me
into a girl deserving of love.

I thought
maybe He was
like you,

but one day I heard His response
as He told me I already was the girl
I had always longed to be.

My Soul Is From a Different Place

faith, hope, grace

The Purpose of Pain

How do you know
that this pain you feel
is darkness tugging
at your soul?

How do you know
that the hurt
is an attack
from your enemies?

Perhaps the pain
is from angels feverishly
sewing thousands of stitches
deep into your spine.

Each stitch meant
to hold wings
firmly in place
for eternity.

And when you stretch
your arms up above your head
the pain becomes almost unbearable.
Almost.

My Soul Is From a Different Place

But you get used to the feeling
and mistakenly believe
it's because pain
is your legacy in life.

When really your soul
is finally learning to adjust
to the power
of its reach.

And when you stretch
your arms again
as wide as they can go,
you can finally embrace God.

Kiss That Scar

Kiss that scar
the one that is jagged, and rough,
the one that you try and hide
because you think that it is ugly.

Rub your palm lovingly
across the hard edges
of its surface,
embrace the design of that scar,
chosen especially for you
by God.

To think only of the pain
when you see that scar
is to forget who you are:
beautiful
strong
filled with compassion
filled with purpose.

The scar does not represent
what you lost,
it shows you all that you gained,
all that you could never
have purchased
with all the riches of the world.

The scar is your awakening,
to you, and everyone who
crosses your path.
It says pay attention,
God showed me where
my heart had been buried.

Kiss that scar
and feel the message,
written out in code,
that only you can decipher.
A secret, shared by God's whisper
into your entire soul,
then spread out into the world
with every beat of your heart.

Our Beautiful Brokenness

What if at the end Jesus says
"Yes, you were right,
they were wrong,
and here is why it does not matter."

What if you could
embrace the warmth of the sun,
feel the pull of the moon,
and see the living waters
of our world,
all from your perch
up on the brightest star.

What if Jesus
brushed your doubts away
like tiny specs of dust
on an old record,
and gave you a new song
to sing instead.

My Soul Is From a Different Place

What if He could
show you His scars
and in them you see
His heartbreak
caused by each one of
your thoughts
of self-doubt.

What if I get to Heaven
and Jesus tells me
that the joke I'd told once,
the one meant to make
people laugh
but only ended up
offending them
really *was* funny.
He got it.

What if He tells me
I'm beautiful,
and does it in such a way
that I'll never
have to look in a mirror again.
Beauty will be seen
in the soul,
not on the face.

What if Jesus tells me
that all those times I cried
and screamed His name,
He was there, holding me.

That if He hadn't been there,
I would have run off,
done something crazy.
But instead, I cried for a while,
dried my tears,
and went back out into
the world that had hurt me.

What if I look back
on my life and see
my brokenness,
my path paved with mistakes,
and Jesus nods proudly
and says,
"Yes! Isn't it beautiful?"

What if the why's
of your life
were answered in an instant,
your understanding
the final gift
that allowed you
to finally feel His grace.

The Smile

The smile,
so brief and sincere
invites me to share my own,

not just with
this stranger
but with someone else.

Another,
like me,
who doubts themselves.

Just when I wonder
how I'll find
that person

how I'll know
that they're in need
of kindness

a voice reminds me
to be
kind to all

that God's work
will be done
by God.

What Is Prayer?

Why do I pray to you?
You, who put each hair on my head,
who made my blue eyes
and strong spirit.

Why do I tell you
what you surely must already know.
Why confess the sins you've seen,
or tell you about my fears?

Do I beg to you?
Do I ask you
to do something
you weren't planning on doing?

Is prayer a reminder
for you to fulfill
promises I perceived
from you?

Is it silent,
from my thoughts and heart,
sent out with emotion
to the only one who'll understand?

Or should prayers be shouted?
Glory! Blessings! As loud and long
as we can to make sure that you know
what it is we're saying.

No.

Prayer is not so you can see me more clearly,
it is how I can see my faults and weaknesses,
and still show my authentic self
to you.

Prayer is not how you know what I desire,
but how I can more freely
see the blessings
from this path you've led me on.

Prayer lets me step out of
our world of time and space
and into your world, our future home,
when we close our eyes and speak with you.

Prayer is our answer
to the questions we have
before we even know
what we would ask.

No Suffering In Heaven

So often
I feel the naivety
of a child
so young and unschooled
at the ways of the world.

The smallest of things,
as others may define them,
confuse me,
bring tears to my eyes,
cause me to fall to the ground
and lament this unsettled world.

There are times when I'm certain
that no one cares about me.

Not one.

Not in the way He does.
Not in the way
that comforts your soul.

As I lay on the ground,
With confusion and despair,
it's His gentleness I seek.

My Soul Is From a Different Place

I long for the day
He pulls me up,
brushes away my fears,
and tells me
it's going to be all right.
Truly.
He's not guessing.
He's seen it all
from beginning to end,
and He knows.

To hear Him tell me
that my naivety was because
I was a visitor here.

To see Him wipe a hand
over my eyes
and dry my tears
forever.

High Regard

He gave her the assignment,
a tough one
because He cherished her.
Her spirit was strong,
but she'd soon forget that
and ask Him why
as tears spilled
from the windows
to her soul.

She'd struggle, feel pain,
and bring the lesson
through for others.

How He valued her!
Holding her tight
even as she wondered
if He really loved her.

Yet she feared leaving here,
Going back
to where her
story began.

My Soul Is From a Different Place

Because she'd forgotten it all,
as she was meant to,
the knowledge she had
siphoned off
as she was pushed through
the confines of time.

Despite her confusion
there were times
when she'd suspected
what her purpose was.

It would sneak up on her
as she made her way
around this life,
doing things she'd deemed
ordinary.

But every once in a while,
she'd feel it,
His nudge,
reminding her of His charge,
telling her about the assignment
and how He would
work through her.

How special she felt!
To be held
in such high regard.

Beacon

Lord,
I'm surrounded by your blessings,
they spread through the air
and keep me cool from the hot glares
of my enemies.

And yet, I struggle.
I can't see beyond this day,
past this hurt and the
harmful words of
those who choose hate.

I don't have the energy
to look back, again.
I've met my past,
embraced my mistakes
and forgiven those who harmed me,
but my house no longer has room
for yesterday.

So where do I turn?
When my future is uncertain
and my past no longer holds me,
which direction shall I walk?

As I bow my head in despair
I hear the voice,
"Look up."

My Soul Is From a Different Place

There is no need to look beyond
what is.
I take the hand He has offered,
close my eyes as I catch my breath,
and feel the light air of blessings
caress my face once again.

He pulls me through,
miles and miles we travel
as I feel the air rush past me.

When I open my eyes,
we are right here,
in the same place as before
but now, I see the beacon
calling me forward.

Call to Me

God,
call out to me
in a voice so loud
I can't mistake it for

my pride
or society's expectations
my parent's guilt
or nosy people who think
they make the rules.

Whisper to me
in a voice so low and certain
I can't pretend it's

just a feeling
a hunch
confusion
or nothing.

Sing to me
in a voice so beautiful
I can't deny

your majesty
your wisdom
the nature of your love
or your infinite grace.

My Soul Is From a Different Place

Talk to me
in a voice so comforting
I can't help

but embrace you
as my friend
my teacher
the divine creator
and the one who made my heart.

The Blessing In My Sleepless Night

It used to be
that sleepless nights
would torment me,
heap worry about the coming day
onto my already burdened mind.

I'd toss and turn angrily,
knowing that each minute
I lay awake
would feel like two in the workday.

I'd wonder how to make
it through a day that
hadn't even
arrived yet.

But God has changed that for me.
While the sleepless nights remain,
He urges me from the bed,
invites me to spend time with Him instead.

In prayer,
I thank Him
for the
blessings.

My Soul Is From a Different Place

Because sleepless nights
in the middle of a beautiful life are small,
and gifts, too plentiful and unrecognized,
loom large over tired eyes.

Instead
of a night spent
fighting with
covers and worried thoughts,

I find comfort
in a bowed head
and prayers
received.

It's as if God has pulled me from my bed
just to spend this time with Him
when the house is quiet
and filled with His grace.

Free Pass

I awake to a dark sky
lighter than night
but subdued and grey,
hiding the sun
and possibility for the day.

Ambitions get washed away,
but the rain and thunder
makes me pause enough
to appreciate that this too
is a gift.

The lighting cracks
the ground,
shakes the house,
reminds me of the One
who is truly in control.

The leaves hold out
their tiny hands
like children,
reaching out to God,
arms extended,

eyes closed,
with smiles that show
their delight

in feeling the rain
upon their faces.

This day
is a free pass
to escape
the driving
pace of an ordinary day.

Cherie Burbach

Every Jagged Edge

I felt you in my heart
but yet doubted that you
would do good by me.

At each disappointment,
I angrily shouted questions,
asking *why me*.

Sometimes, I would pause,
remain still,
and know that you were there.

I'd see those rare times,
when the big things in my life
were as were should be.

But before long, pain would return,
and along with it,
my questions about you.

My anger paused only long enough
to feel the shame
of my disbelief.

I moved easily
between great love and admiration
to bitterness and guilt.

My Soul Is From a Different Place

I thought maybe you *were* great,
as great as I'd heard,
but not for me.

Others would receive your grace,
but I wasn't good enough for it,
or so I believed.

But you persisted,
undaunted by my childish ways,
you refused to leave my heart.

And I matured
in the understanding
of your word.

I could be with you
without hiding
from my imperfection.

My beautiful brokenness
laid open to you,
the one who'd seen it all along.

My arms stretched open,
my face turned up,
surrendering to your love.

My mistakes, fears,
and every jagged edge
caressed by your grace.

Finally, I looked back at the anger and doubt,
and felt the weight of shame
upon my soul.

I thought of the tears
cried out to you,
asking where you were.

I remembered
the pleading, the begging,
for the course of my life to change.

I saw gratitude only after blessings were granted,
and not before,
in anticipation of them.

I bowed my head in apology,
and heard your voice:
Thank you for your honest prayers.

I realized then
there was no need to return to you
because you had never left me.

You Have Seen Us Through

Dear Lord
Please blow your gentle breath
on the clouds
that have overstayed
their winter welcome.

Ask them to part,
letting the sun reveal
the beauty
that's been hiding
these long cold months.

It's time we
showed our faces.
Let us learn
from the tulips
that will boldly
lead the way,
punching through
the protection of snow
they no longer need.

Let us stand
as courageously
as they,
unafraid of

the harshness of a world
that may not be ready
for our arrival.

Let us be like
the crocus,
practical and diverse,
showing the world
their variety of colors,
their saffron treasure
rare and distinct.

Let us offer
similar gifts,
exquisite and valuable,
adding such unique flavor
to the world
that it cannot be duplicated
by anyone else.

Let us run wild
like the daffodils,
claiming space through
the meadows and woods,
their yellow and orange shades
reminding us of
the life force
in our sun.

My Soul Is From a Different Place

Dear Lord,
melt the snow
and erase the coldness
from our hearts.

As the flowers
mark the arrival
of brighter days,
filled with warmth
and beauty,
let us turn our faces
to the sky,
raise our arms, and rejoice,
for you have seen us
through the darkness of winter.

This Is What I Crave

And this is what I crave
these quiet moments
when I can
turn down
the pace of this life
and listen to my Lord.

This is what I long for
these creative moments
when I can
paint the joy
in being a
beautiful,
strong,
grateful
child of God.

This is what I've yearned for
these humble moments
when I can
finally understand
the love God has for me,
now and from the minute
He placed his spirit in my heart.

My Soul Is From a Different Place

This is what I've hungered for
these soulful moments
when I can
place pen to paper
and feel my purpose.

I See God

I see God
in the smile that comes
suddenly and unexpectedly
from a stranger,

just when I think
I'm not worthy,
my failures and ineptitude
so far reaching

that they
cloak my face
yet leave
my body naked.

Just then
when I think
God has forgotten
about me

as I walk
through a crowd
surrounded by others
who are all too deserving

My Soul Is From a Different Place

of love and gratitude
and thus,
more important
to God,

the face of a stranger
rushes by
yet stops,
for a moment,

as our eyes meet
and my existence
is validated
as if to say

I see you
and
you're important
to Him.

My Soul Is From a Different Place

My soul is from a different place
it remembers the day
God placed it gently within this body
that had yet to form.

It tugs at me sometimes
filling me with longing
as it whispers about a place
beyond this world.

It tries to explain the concept of freedom
as I close my eyes, arms wide,
and feel the warmth of the sun
caress my face.

My soul pushes me to connect
while I hesitate,
remember nothing but rejection
as it nudges me toward new friends.

My soul is from a different place,
and one day it will guide me back there,
where He will tell me,
"Welcome home."

My Soul Is From a Different Place

About the Author:

Cherie Burbach is a freelance writer specializing in lifestyle and relationships. She's written for About.com, NBC/Universal, Match.com, Philips Lifeline, and more.

Whether it's writing about caregiving, finding love, or making new friends, all of Cherie's fiction and nonfiction centers around relationships and faith.

Cherie's poetry reflects the faith and hope that is evident in her life story. Her nonfiction books help people connect, meet new people, and find balance in their lives.

For more on Cherie, visit her website, cherieburbach.com.

A Note of Thanks

I published my first book of poetry, *The Difference Now*, a decade ago. What a life changing event that was.

Back then, I was first starting to come out of my "poetry shell" and feeling confident enough to put a book together just for me. Up until then, I destroyed much of what I wrote. So I wanted to prove to myself that I could gather together the poems I wrote and produce a book from them.

But what happened next was amazing, and the reason for this note of thanks. Readers responded. You bought the book, and I'm so amazed and grateful for that. You wrote me, telling me how you related to the words. You encouraged me. Many of you told me you enjoyed my work, and the way you have shared your stories with me is such a blessing.

Poetry is subjective. Some people will find peace and hope in these words. Some will take them and apply them to their own situation. Some will feel God's grace, while others will find a word or two that stays with them days after.

And some readers just won't relate. Their experience is from a completely different perspective and they won't like it or get it. And that's perfectly okay.

In fact, if you read this book and didn't like it… well, I'm sorry for that. But please, keep reading poetry until you find a poet that speaks to you. Poetry is too valuable not to try again to find something you love.

If you did enjoy this book, I hope you'll seek out my other titles, and tell a friend who you think might enjoy it also.

If you're a blogger, please write a post or review, as these are very hard to come by as an author (and even more difficult as a poet!).

If you'd like to contact me with any questions or feedback, you'll find me here: http://cherieburbach.com/contact/.

Thanks for picking up this book and for traveling this decade-long journey with me.

www.ingramcontent.com/pod-product-compliance
Lightning Source LLC
Chambersburg PA
CBHW031455040426
42444CB00007B/1108